Feeling Therapy:
Real Health: Yourself

Feeling Therapy: Real Health: Yourself

Jack Waddington

authorHOUSE®

AuthorHouse™ LLC
1663 Liberty Drive
Bloomington, IN 47403
www.authorhouse.com
Phone: 1-800-839-8640

Published by AuthorHouse   02/19/2014

ISBN: 978-1-4918-6360-2 (sc)
ISBN: 978-1-4918-6359-6 (e)

Contents

Acknowledgments

Jim Sauerbier, my lover for 18 years, who is today my best friend and loving companion.

I need to acknowledge the enormous amount of time, energy, and enthusiasm my editor put into this book: Robert Clover Johnson, retired research editor for Gallaudet University, Washington, DC, and practitioner of various forms of feeling therapy.

One of the inspirations for writing this book was when a couple of respondents on Art Janov's blog asked, how might it be possible to offer a therapy to those not able to get Los Angeles or not able to afford it even if they were here.?

I gave this great thought because of the enormous diversity of people, having varying abilities to feel and in need of help to express feelings. It seemed a daunting task. I knew what I was going to propose would be controversial, but I decided to give it a try anyway.

Warning

This book is not for the casual reader or for those who read it superficially and decide to give it a try. It was written to help those who have been interested in Primal Therapy and have read at least *The Primal Scream* and feel the need to do this therapy because they are suffering. It is not an easy or even intuitive read. It is intended for those who have thought for some time, "If only I had the money and could get to Los Angeles."

Should you start to get into your feelings and then realize this is more than you bargained for, there is a relatively easy way to back out. Resume your lifestyle (defenses and act-outs) as it was before you read about or tried to get into feelings. This was how you naturally dealt with feelings in the past, and that approach will stand you in good stead as a way *out* of your feelings.

There is nothing intrinsically harmful in feelings, but after many years of defending and acting-out, experiencing previously repressed feelings can be very disturbing. Any attempt to sue because you discover that you have set out on something more intense than you expected would not be appropriate. It is important for you to study this book thoroughly and read at least some of the other books I recommend before embarking on this journey. And it is important to take care to learn just how much deep feelings you are able to tolerate safely in any given session. It will be your sole responsibility to do so and consequently there should be no grounds for a lawsuit.

Prologue

The discovery of Primal Pain led to the development by Arthur Janov of Primal Theory, which endeavors to explain the dynamics of modern humans' neurotic existence. In this brief volume, I begin by summarizing Primal Theory succinctly so that the reader can begin to grasp the principles underlying what I choose to call *Feeling Therapy*. Many who read this book may already be aware of some of those principles from reading Arthur Janov's first and most famous book, *The Primal Scream*.

It is my belief that if enough people were to begin experiencing Primal Pain in accord with the principles of Primal Theory, future generations could benefit from having parents less likely to inflict needless trauma on their children. Under those circumstances, I believe, human beings in general would be less neurotic. Eventually, we could return to a more natural, healthful state and regain our original "Feeling-full" humanity. My purpose here is to suggest that the more honesty and connectedness we have concerning our true, underlying feelings, the healthier we will be.

This is not an easy ride. The longer we have been away from expressing ourselves simply, naturally, and directly, the more difficult it is to get back to doing so with any degree of ease.

We all know deep down that there is something amiss, but we are not sure what it is. Hence, we are forever floundering to find solutions. I hope in this book to demonstrate the problem and make suggestions as to how we might fix it, but be forewarned: This is a slow and often painful process. It will require quite a lot of devotion, patience, and endurance. Not a simple ride, Feeling Therapy has many pitfalls and plateaus where progress will seem impossible.

In the end, though, I and many others who have pursued this course are convinced it is worth it. You will probably experience great relief as pent up feelings are finally expressed and periods of astonishment as life patterns based on those repressed feelings become clearer and less compulsively binding. Nevertheless, there is no "final goal" (end game) to this process: merely life as one travels through it, traveled in a more natural, genuine, enlightened way.

Introduction

Sometime around the mid-nineteen-sixties I attended a clinic in London, England for a penicillin injection. On getting the injection I suddenly felt a rush of adrenaline through my body and within seconds my heart was pounding so fast I feared it might burst. Then suddenly, there was a tearing sensation in the back of my neck. I fell to the floor screaming at the top of my lungs, "I'm dying, I'm dying." I didn't even know I had that kind of scream in me. I was seized by terror like I'd never known before. I had no idea what was happening to me, but knew I was in a situation of enormous vulnerability.

Seconds later, I felt that tearing sensation in the back of my neck again. The terror now mounted to a height that I didn't know was possible. This second phase felt like I was now in outer space. I was terrified and truly felt my life was on the line. I looked up at the doctor as I was being put on an examination table. His face was green (I exaggerate not) and his hair was standing on end: "Jesus," I thought, "if that's how scared the doctor is, what the hell is going on with me?" He seemed to have no idea what was going on with me either.

Then there was another tearing sensation at the back of my neck. If the second one took me into outer space, I now felt I'd left the universe completely. I didn't believe it was possible to experience this amount of terror and live.

Then suddenly, I was a baby in my cot (crib) and could see the wall and ceiling above me. On the wall was a "Mickey Mouse" tricycle hanging over a gas bracket above the fireplace. The colors were unbelievably vivid; the taste in my mouth was unlike anything I'd known in my life to that point and I was screaming for my life. Some moments later, I was transposed to another scene where I was a baby crawling on the floor. I felt so small or rather the room felt so large. The carpet was familiar but the room wasn't. At that point the doctor was injecting me with some tranquilizer to quiet me down. I was indeed brought down from that scene to being outside the universe.

This incident was so devastating that it stayed with me for several years. Then in 1973 I picked up *The Primal Scream*. On reading the introduction, I was an instant convert. I threw the book in the air and exclaimed, "I've got it," i.e. the clinic incident now made total sense to me. I couldn't put the book down and read it in two days. After reading it, I read it again just to make sure I had got it right. Within another two days, I had re-read it.

This clinic experience was so profound, but at the time I was not able, in-spite of many insights about myself, to make total sense of it. After reading *The Primal Scream* it all started to fall into place for me. I was not quite sure why or how until I had done a fair amount of therapy at the Primal Institute. But I was, without doubt, an instant convert after reading *The Primal Scream*. I have never looked back since, and spent the better part of the last 30 years doing Primal Therapy. It is the time spent there and on my own therapy that gives me the strong incentive to writing this book.

PART I
THE THEORY

The reason for offering Primal Theory is to demonstrate to the reader my premise for this book.

The discovery I mentioned in the prologue was made by Dr. Arthur Janov, a psychologist who had been working for seventeen years in private practice in Los Angeles. After watching two of his patients writhing on the floor for several minutes, in separate sessions and listening to the tape he made of them, many times, Janov named this discovery "Primal Pain." He defined Primal Pain as the pain that resided within every neurotic from early childhood. This he recounted in the introduction of his famous best-selling book *The Primal Scream*.

Earlier, others had noted that pain from our past resides within us and affects us for the rest of our lives. Sigmund Freud acknowledged its presence and impact. Others had suggested that all events in our past were stored intact in our memories though they did not make clear why this was so, or what their effects were. Janov had studied many related ideas, but was somewhat dissatisfied with then current explanations.

On seeing his patients go through what he, Janov, recognized as a "reliving" of a painful early childhood event and the impact on the patients, he diligently set about, over the next several months, to explain it in psychological terms. Having a Ph.D. in neurophysiology, he was well equipped to formulate a consistent theory which has been verified both objectively and subjectively with thousands of primal patients over the last 40 years.

In Part I of this book I attempt to reiterate Primal Theory in my own words. Janov explains it more fully in the first 80 pages of *The Primal Scream*. I merely wish to restate it briefly.

1

Neurosis

(the problem)

Janov defined neurosis as the pathology of feeling. When feelings are not fully accessible (a pathological condition), then we are neurotic. Freud, being a neuro-physician, coined the word "neurosis", but did not adequately define it. Not until Janov and *The Primal Scream* was neurosis fully defined. It was the genius of Janov and the simplicity of his definition that gave us insight as to how the brain (mind) works. Janov stated that we create the subconscious (Freud called it the unconscious) to store unfelt pain and intimated that all that is contained in the subconscious is unfelt pain. He further stated that if this subconscious pain could be re-lived, as opposed to remembered, it would then be reconnected to the conscious mind. Consequently, both neurosis and many of the mysteries of the subconscious could be potentially demystified.

How many of us are neurotic? I feel none of us escape it. I contend that we all know deep down there is something amiss, though we are never quite sure what. That mysterious something is primal pain. Our inability to access this pain *is* neurosis.

2

Need

Janov stated that we are all born needing, as I feel all other creatures are. Our needs are relatively simple and most creatures know this instinctively. As newborns we need to breathe freely, be fed when we need nourishment, to be held, kept clean and warm. We need to feel safe and develop in our own way and time. In other words, we need to be loved. Often we humans confuse need with want. Unmet wants may produce frustration but not disastrous consequences. Unmet needs, on the other hand, are catastrophic and affect us for the rest of our lives unless we are able to finally feel them and respond to them. Need implies that if it is unmet, we will suffer enormous consequences.

3

Pain

When needs go unmet, we feel pain. As children we feel *overwhelming pain* when our needs go unmet because we have little or no resources to alleviate pain. We are totally reliant on our caregiver (mother usually). Babies and very young children invariably cry when they feel pain. A baby or young child crying is in pain, contrary to some notions that babies and young children cry for effect and manipulation, or worse, just as a way to breathe or let off steam. This is a tragic myth.

The pain does not go away. It just gets stored in the subconscious.

Many use the word "Pain" in the primal community with respect to their early feelings but I feel this word is bandied around way too glibly. Feelings are not in-and-of-themselves painful when they are expressed. It is the holding back on letting those feeling out and expressing them that is painful and further causes a great deal of tension (energy) to hold them back.

It was our inability to express our feelings in childhood that created the repressed pain. This pain then stays for a life-time until felt and expressed.

4

Feelings

A feeling is a psychophysical event or sensation within our bodies. There are many feelings and sensations and most of them we experience in early childhood and many we carry into adulthood . . . like hunger, touch, urination and defecation, and of course pain. However, we commonly think of feelings and emotions as the same. Janov made a very clear distinction between the two and I concur with Janov's definition. An emotion (as the word is defined) is an expression of a feeling. This suggests there are two components to all feelings: first, the physical sensation and then, the emotional response, the latter indicating that the mind participates in the expression. Examples of the use of these components in a feeling experience are: if you are pricked with a pin, the feeling is a pin prick; the emotion is usually: "ouch." Another instance would be if you feel sad (have the sensation of sadness), the response (emotion) could be to cry.

In childhood the whole feeling spectrum is available to the child (unless already severely damaged). It is those feelings that as adults we tend to repress (deliberately or otherwise), perhaps for reasons we consider childish. That is what I hope in this book to dispel.

5

Memory

Our ability to remember is fundamental to our existence since remembering experiences will determine how we react to similar events in the future. The problem arises when we don't have total access to all our memories. Yet, it is suggested they are all there intact somewhere. A medical example would be amnesia after a traumatic event, like a horrific road accident. A traumatic experience in a child's life from an unmet need also results in amnesia relating to that event.

Repressed memories are not totally lost to us, but to bring them fully back to memory and totally back to consciousness is another matter. Repression is the loss of access to all or part of the memory, but not the feeling, which remains '*reverberating*' within our bodies until it is fully felt.

6

The Subconscious

Freud used the word "unconscious" rather than "subconscious." The use of "unconscious" for me suggests the loss of consciousness on many or all levels—knocked out. While there may be good reasons for using "unconscious" in psychology, I would prefer to use the word "subconscious" because it suggests *under* the conscious level rather than nowhere to be found. I will therefore refer to it as the subconscious from here on.

I suggest that there are two forms of consciousness: one we are aware of and one we are only subliminally aware of—the subconscious. Most of us are aware of something beyond the conscious mind, but we know not what. We humans throughout time have speculated on many notions about this, which I feel accounts for our mythologies and belief systems.

Janov suggested that our ability as humans to cut off from, and relegate traumatic pain to an area of the brain was a necessary part of our species' survivability, especially in childhood. It seems that no other creatures have this faculty. We could call it "the split," "repression" or the "subconscious." It is an act of denial until it is re-lived. Janov intimated that all the subconscious contains *is* repressed pain.

7

The Defense System

Once a feeling has been relegated to the subconscious, Janov states, it remains there '*reverberating*,' seeking an outlet for expression. When it finds a potential outlet, it starts to surface into consciousness, usually triggered by a similar feeling in the present. It is at this point that we consciously begin to steer clear of upcoming feelings of pain. None of us like pain and instinctively will do our utmost to avoid it, and make it go away. However, in this case we are steering clear of an already resident feeling, *but* are not fully aware of it.

As adults, we have many means of deflecting upcoming pain. In psychology these are called "defenses" or "act-outs." There is one other called an "act-in," but I will go into that in the chapter on medicine. Some take pain-killing drugs or alcohol; others overeat or overindulge in other things like over-working, gambling or excessive sex.

It is our individual, deep-rooted means of defense that keeps us locked into neurosis for a lifetime. Psychology has suggested different act-outs (defenses) to be different disorders. Primal Theory *implies* they are just different manifestations (symptoms) of the same disorder: namely neurosis.

The neurotic is subconsciously forever trying to resolve the hurt (trauma) of the past, by reproducing it in the present in order (hopefully and subconsciously) to resolve it. This never works, but the habit persists.

In Summary

Overwhelmed by pain, the child instinctively disconnects from its memory through a process commonly called amnesia from pain; the child is left disconnected from its memory. However this subliminal pain does not go away, but is forever left *reverberating* in the subconscious. When a similar feeling in later life is brought forward nature attempts to heal itself by triggering a re-living of the earlier trauma, but because of the sheer magnitude of the original trauma we repress it vehemently. Hence, we set up defenses (act-outs).

PART II

THE IMPLICATIONS

Primal Theory was and still is the only psychological theory since Freud. Many have challenged the efficacy of it, but not from any sound basis as far as I am aware; and based their notions on the efficacy of the *therapy*.

I challenge anyone to do so. It has stood the test of the last 40 years and has been validated. Because of this, I contend, there are implications.

No one has a monopoly on feelings. Each of us has some (subliminal) awareness of their existence, but unearthing and expressing those feelings is the key to achieving 'real' health. In summary; the theory states that we as babies have needs which, if not fully met, cause us to suffer *overwhelming pain* which we then have to repress by splitting the memory of those events from our consciousness. Unfortunately, this split from consciousness means we have no access through memory to those events, but are forever left floundering and only subliminally aware that something is amiss. Later in life, we develop defense mechanisms to prevent current feelings from triggering us to re-experience these deeper primal feelings. These defenses then become embedded and reinforced as we get older. Primal Theory suggests that nothing short of a **re-living** of the original event will connect it back into our consciousness, thus causing the defense mechanisms to cease to be effective or necessary.

Neurosis, as Janov defines it, serves the purpose of defending ourselves from the initial (primal) pain. In childhood, that defense was necessary for survival, but as we grew older, and better able to survive, 'defenses' act against us, causing characteristics within us that we would really like to be without. The alternative is to re-live the pain the defense system guards against. Alas, we instinctively run away from *any and all pain*. We then become prisoners of this pain as Janov noted well in his book *Prisoners of Pain*.

Until the discovery of Primal Pain and the underlying theory explaining it, we humans have been endeavoring to explain that "*something in the back of our minds.*" Primal Theory identifies the problem and further implies that we humans are not that unique as creatures on the planet. Our uniqueness turns out to be a *debilitating disorder* that we would be better and healthier without. There are those of us who will have easier access to feelings than others.

Life circumstances and careers do play a part in all this and there are many careers that are more neurotic (less feeling-full) than others. The military is by far the worst for it is involved in killing other humans; the police force comes a close second, then prison wardens. Next are animal experimenters, then politicians and all professions involved in telling others how they ought to behave: rabbis, priests, religious ministers, etc.

All of us possess within ourselves the means to bring about our own health, life, and emotional prosperity. It is the process of accessing it that makes this exercise in feeling and expressing feelings so elusive . . . but not impossible. We were all born with this ability fully formed, but sadly, due to the childrearing we receive, we had it taken away from us. It remains there, but it takes a real effort (not in a rational, cognitive manner) to allow our bodies, through feelings, to tell us where and how far to go. Trust your gut feeling; it is your best guide.

Part II of this book is my attempt to describe this process, BUT we are each unique, so it is within our differences that we are going to have to navigate. Again, I must emphasize; this is not an easy journey.

If you are able to afford Primal therapy and are able to give time to practicing it with a trained Primal therapist, I highly recommend you do so. However, this book is meant for those desperate to improve the quality of their lives who for one reason or another cannot afford that approach.

Take your time. This process cannot be rushed. There are no shortcuts and beware of those who offer their services without credentials. Initially, this therapy can be daunting. Pursuing it is by nature a new way of being. Again, *trust your gut feeling*. If anything feels wrong, discontinue that particular approach until such time as you feel more confident in it.

Feeling feelings does not necessitate re-living them.

In Part II I mentioned that re-living the feeling was the only way to bring it back into consciousness. In this book I am not suggesting that you attempt to re-live old feelings. If that happens in its own good way and time, 'all well and good', **but you should not make that a goal**. To do so could be catastrophic. What I am recommending, in essence, is that you aim to feel what is going on in your body and to express that feeling *as best you know how*.

Feeling your feelings will bring you far closer to **real** health than repressing the expression of feelings. Try not to think of this as a sort of perfection. I am merely suggesting that you gracefully, and *as best you can and know how*, express the feelings you feel, and be confident that this brings you closer to health than all the alternatives out there.

8

The Mind

In a general way, we all know what the mind is and does, but specifically the mind is the physiology of the brain. By physiology we mean the workings of the brain. The workings of the brain contain many factors, not least of which are the automatic aspects of living like the heartbeat and the digestive processes and the instinctive reactions. What I want to discuss are the conscious and subconscious aspects of the mind.

The conscious mind

The conscious aspect is, for the most part understandable insofar as we sense it. Some of the conscious aspects of the mind such as walking, working, talking, and thinking seem normal, but how many of these are intrinsic to our being? Walking and working I suggest are, but talking is something that was developed at a much later time in our evolution. To demonstrate my point there is the story of a human baby left in the desert, picked up and raised by a gazelle. The child eventually learned to run and catch up with other gazelles, but it never learned to talk, which suggests that talking is not intrinsic. I understand there are many other such examples.

The subconscious mind

I suggested in Chapter 6 what the subconscious is. The subconscious is the most elusive part of the mind, and we humans have been concerned about it for eons by virtue of our lack of access to it. As I suggested earlier, the split away from the conscious mind that creates the subconscious acted initially as a survival mechanism in our early childhood development. Later, because of repression, the subconscious acted as a barrier to fully seeing ourselves in a total context and left us only with defensive mechanisms we never fully understood. As adults we are left with this legacy, hindering our ability to get the most out of life. Just being aware of this aspect of the total mind might, I contend, be our greatest clue to unraveling many factors that religious, spiritual, philosophical and political thinkers have toyed with for centuries, never quite getting to the core of the matter that we have been seeking.

The implications

I contend that all other creatures communicate with their own kind and with other species through the expression of their feelings. These expressions are most often noises made vocally, but can also be body movements and postures (including facial expressions). I contend that somewhere in our past, we did exactly the same thing with grunts, groans, crying, and laughing. This I feel preceded language as we now know it. Language is something we learn from others; we are not born with it. Consequently, language is not intrinsic to our nature, but vocal expressions of our feelings *were and are*. It is our inability (because of neurosis) to fully express our feelings that has left us unaware of the very nature of feelings. In essence, I contend that neurotics are only subliminally aware of some sensations—some of us more than others; depending on the level of repression in childhood.

Ways to envision the subconscious

Some ways to envision the subconscious might be: first, as a normal part of consciousness that splits away from the rest anatomically through the synapses (nerve endings in the brain). A great deal of work has been done in this area—mentioned at great length in Janov's many other books—that seems to be in accord with Janov's postulation. A second way of viewing the subconscious is as a blocking mechanism by us humans to deal with pain that was overwhelming to us as children. A third way would be as the part of the mind which subjectively denies that the feeling exists, in order not to feel it. In all cases, we sacrifice the ability to remember that event—we repress the memory. Hence it takes something as drastic as a *re-living* of the event to reconnect it back into consciousness or, put another way, to reconnect the synapses that created the split.

A thought about thoughts

Our human history, even those very vague remnants of it we see through archeology, takes us back no further than 20,000-30,000 years. In terms of our history as humans (homo sapiens) there were more than 80,000 years prior to that. What were we really like during that whole 80,000 year period? Our early writings, drawings, architecture and monuments tell us little about the social life of humans. It is obvious that we could do tasks and carry things, but at what point were we able to think?

Contemplate the concept

I ask you to contemplate this as a possible scenario without immediately attempting to dismiss it. If we can stretch to this point, then most of the rest will fall into place. I feel that most who read *The Primal Scream* were reluctant to accept the notion of hidden feelings. So, why did some accept this, and yet many didn't? My contention is that it either touched on some deep feelings within us, or it didn't. If it did, we pursued further; if not, then it was merely just another idea.

Why my experience in that London clinic was important to me.

In my case, the London clinic incident stuck in my memory. From time to time, I was acutely aware that I had had an experience that I was not able to rationalize. I reasoned, in hindsight, that from the moment of being tranquilized, I did not complete the experience. I had many deep insights afterwards, but had I been allowed to complete the whole experience, I might have come to a similar conclusion as Janov did. Not that I would have been able to formulate Primal Theory: I did not have the background to conceive this, but I know I would have known a deeper self. Others that I have met contend that *The Primal Scream* made great sense to them because, in almost all cases, it touched upon their subliminal feeling that there was something demonstrated by this unshakeable notion.

There is something unsatisfactory about life as we experience it now.

I can only appeal to the conscious mind and to the broader population's sense that there is something unsatisfactory with the way we are conducting life right now. I feel there is general dissatisfaction with the way most of us spend our lives. Where did all the joy and excitement go? I am not suggesting that life should always be pleasant and joyful, but when most of it for most of us, is unpleasant, or at best just boring drudgery, surely there is something amiss. Why do so many of us now need to take antidepressants? There are many suggestions afloat as to how we might improve matters, but it is evident that most of these are 'band-aids' and do not get to the core problem—said another way, we do not get to the *Center of the Cyclone* as suggested by John C. Lilly in his book of that name.

Things are getting much too complicated, like simply just doing and understanding the tax system. It appears we need a Ph.D. in rocket science just to program our mobile (cell) phones. Computers are not that simple or intuitive to use either and leave many of us frustrated much of the time. We get the same feeling in medicine. Most of us refuse to even try and think in scientific terms. It's all rapidly becoming too complicated. I endeavor to rec-tify some of this by proffering Primal Theory in Part I as a new way to look at ourselves and the life we are involved in, since for the most part, the spiritual, political, and rational modalities seem **not** to have given us any real overall answers.

At the back of our minds

If we are able to visualize that the conscious mind has a hidden component and all it contains is stored pain, I feel that is all we need to be aware of. We are not totally unaware of the subconscious, but merely think of it as *somewhere in the back of our minds*. Sadly, we jump upon any suggestion that offers an explanation and we will believe many myths in order to reinforce our beliefs. Our known history of the human race (at best 10,000 years) is a testimony to just this. I will endeavor to look into some of these reckonings in the course of this book. We all know deep down there is something amiss. This something, I contend, has baffled us humans throughout our known history as evidenced by the mythologies which we still embrace to this day.

If thinking is done through language, as suggested by Benjamin Lee Whorf in 1944, in *Language, Mind, and Reality*, it might indicate that before neurosis we did not think in the same manner that we currently do. It is in this sense that we know animals do not think in the way that **we** think. (Feeling is another state of being) Sure, animals use the left side of their brain to organize and express their feeling, but that is a far different matter than concocting mathematics. We initially merely reacted to feelings using the brain (mind) as do all other creatures on the planet. Thinking is a recently-learned habit in terms of our evolution. The mind does way more things than just think and create ideas.

9

Feelings and Emotions

(emotions being the expression of feelings)

These two words are not synonyms

A "feeling" is a psychophysical event. An "emotion" is an expression of a feeling.

The nature of feelings is not a mystery, and all of us have them in varying degrees of awareness. Feelings happen to us willy-nilly and contrary to some, we have no control over them. What we do have control over is how we express them (the emotions). This **controlling** factor is: neurosis.

Neurosis and its unhealthiness

Freud coined the word neurosis. It was Janov, however, who offered a workable definition of neurosis in *The Primal Scream*. What he stated was that it is our reluctance to express feelings that makes us unhealthy.

Getting back to health: physically and mentally

Is there a way to get our health back OTHER THAN Primal therapy? The term "Primal therapy" refers specifically to the therapy devised and used by Arthur Janov in his center and refers to a very special therapist/ patient relationship methodology. This book is my attempt to offer a do-it-yourself use of feelings for a better health and to show how that might be achieved. Getting into feelings and their expression as I describe them here IS NOT Primal therapy, per se, but the approach I recommend can carry us on a similar journey towards better health, by permitting feelings and expressing them *as best we know how*. "Feeling Therapy," as I call it, is not easy and is very time-consuming and there is no "**end point**" in the quest for feelings and expressing them. Once started, one is on a journey for life to be 'feeling-full', and remain feeling-full rather than acting-out feelings (defending against feelings) and leaving ourselves open to all the consequences of living life neurotically (unhealthily).

There are many who will not see the purpose of striving to be feeling-full; This book is not written for those people.

However there are many whose lives are threatened by rising pain, who perhaps have read *The Primal Scream,* or Janov's other books, and who wish they could alleviate some of the devastating, ongoing, debilitating feelings of these rising pains. This book is definitely for those people.

As stated in Part I, these pains are a result of old pains from the womb, infant-hood, and early childhood, rising up within our selves and debilitating our very being. Nature, in-and-of-itself, tends to try to heal our wounds; the rising pain is nature's way of trying to heal our inner selves. However, the ensuing pain is something most of us had to squelch in early childhood; hence, we will do whatever it takes to prevent it from rising. "*Neurosis is self-perpetuating.*" Primal Therapy made the promise to get us beyond that reluctance to feel and express it. Most of those who have come to do Primal Therapy did so on that promise. However, there must be millions out there who would love to enter into that fold and conquer this debilitating disease called neurosis. This book is my attempt to offer a "*do it yourself* . . . Feel your way to health.

The Pitfalls

Let me say from the get-go: There are many potential pitfalls in this process and I wish to clearly outline as many of these as I can think of. What that means is that the reader needs to understand very clearly these potential pitfalls, which suggests that a superficial reading **will not** be sufficient.

Many years ago, I undertook "The Frederick Maithers Alexander technique." I attended sessions with one of that method's practitioners and later read one of Alexander's books: *The Use of the Self.* He was asked if it was possible for anyone to learn this 'technique' through just reading his book. He replied, "Yes, if they could read," hinting that most of us were not able to read with any depth. I am tempted to suggest the very same response. It will require that any reader wishing to partake of this "*do it yourself*" book will need to have to read it carefully, and perhaps re-read it, to be fully aware (cognizant) of what is being proposed.

Once started, the process and progress is not that straightforward either. There are plateaus and times when progress seems to be elusive. Much perseverance is required, and knowing that we are not talking about weeks or months . . . but perhaps years.

The rewards, when they do occur, are clear. They are, *in my opinion*, well worth it, and offer a rewarding life of reasonable health, and many clear ideas about life.

There are no two humans who suffer rising pain the same way.

In a book of this nature it is almost impossible to touch on all the permutations of different ways pain surfaces within us. Therefore, I can only generalize about the more obvious categories.

I ask the reader to bear this in mind, and suggest that each person attempting to get into feelings on their own must become aware **of their own uniqueness** and **TRUST their own feelings**. *This is easier said than done*, and for those **who have little self esteem** the process can be devastatingly difficult. BUT as best you can, trust your body's sensations and refrain as much as possible from "***trying to figure it out in your head***." Becoming aware of your feelings is by its very nature a bodily process . . . ***not a reasoning one.***

Subsequent Chapters

The subsequent chapters are an attempt to break the process down into the different experiences that each of us have. Some are more devastating than others and none of them are easy.

10

Sadness

(predominant and/or just intermittent)

This chapter is directed toward those who feel a seemingly permanent and persistent sadness about almost everything that happens to them in life, or who suffer from this feeling intermittently. This sadness has its roots in early childhood, infanthood and sometimes womb life. What one must resist is trying to *'figure out'* where and when that occurred. Once you have expressed sufficient sadness, by whatever is your own way of expressing sadness (usually crying; and yes, men do cry), the feeling itself will permit you to descend deeper and deeper into your own history and insights will occur naturally. The source of your sadness will make total sense to you and **only** to you. It is *your* feeling and it belongs *only to you.* It is for this reason that a therapist without sufficient training in Primal Therapy can be very dangerous, trying to make suggestions and guiding you to *their* idea of what *your* insights should be. As a person experiencing your feelings, you are sovereign unto yourself, and I emphasize: your insights apply **solely** to you.

In the early stages of attempting to stay with your feelings, in this case sadness, it may seem that crying, or your way of expressing your sadness (maybe sobbing) is difficult, even to the point of impossible, even though for most of us in childhood, crying was relatively intuitive. Because of the intervening years of repressing the expression of sadness we lose the ability to respond simply, easily, and intuitively.

Attempt to stay with this feeling and expression as long as you are able to sob or cry, **your way.** Each time you go into your feeling, stay with it as long as you can. This will get easier as time progresses, but refrain from trying to rush the process. To use the Frederick Maithers Alexander technique phrase, "**let it happen.**" More easily said than done, I admit, but as best you can, **trust your bodily feelings** (your "gut" feelings) and, again, try to refrain from "figuring them out." Let the feelings tell you all you need to know and, during each session, stay with the feelings and permit them to take you where they will. Be patient with yourself. *It is not always easy to feel.*

Feeling sessions or (another way of saying it) "being on the floor"

Feeling sessions involve going into yourself. Lay down on a carpeted floor, mattress, with or without cushions. Be as physically comfortable as you can be. Ideally, do this in a room with no distractions from windows or from neighbors overhearing you. I recommend subdued lighting (curtains drawn to keep out excessive light). If you do this at night in bed alone, that can often be more convenient, but this may not always be practical for everyone. It is not imperative to be on the floor, but I feel that doing so facilitate feelings.

If *your* crying or sobbing is likely to be overheard by roommates or neighbors, try crying or sobbing into a pillow to avoid attracting attention. This can sometimes feel stifling, but is better than nothing.

It can often feel frustrating and sometimes bewildering, but best you can, '*let it happen.*' As I stated earlier in this chapter, things don't go in straight lines. It is only after a considerable amount of time that some things begin to make sense, and perhaps also sensing that the feelings are not quite as intense as they used to be. These are the moments when you begin to realize the great benefits of feeling and expressing feelings.

Sadness tends to be easier for females, but that is not to say that males should not attempt to get into their sadness's. I find sadness the easiest of the feelings *to feel and express* and crying does a great deal for me, even when there is little by way of connecting to my history. There are many moments for me when the present is also very sad.

You will not always feel overwhelmed with sadness, but even so it is expedient to be on the floor, if you can, feeling and expressing your sadness. A time may come when it may seem unnecessary to be on the floor and feel. I suggest you resist that feeling and get on the floor anyway. Over time you will, *as I keep repeating*, feel the benefits and the healthfulness of expressing your feelings.

"Cure By Crying"
I highly recommend this book by Thomas A. Stone, published in 1995. He made an audiotape of the book. I have some reservations about the book, the main one being that he did not re-state Primal Theory. Though he acknowledged Janov, I feel he did not give him sufficient

credit for his discovery of Primal Pain, nor for his formulation for Primal theory.

I also feel that he somewhat overemphasized the crying response. There are other responses to feeling, like anger and rage. Though these feelings might eventually get down to crying, it may be necessary to start off by expressing one's anger. It gave me pause to write this book in light of Stone's book, which I find very thorough, but my book is much more succinct, a fact which has benefits. I also felt the need to explain some of the more far-reaching aspects of feelings and their expression. Nevertheless, *Cure by Crying* is a great book for those wishing to feel on their own and use my book as an auxiliary text.

If sadness is not predominant

Even though you may not be feeling sad most of the time, it is the same process if and when those sad feelings arise. Lie down and feel them and express them . . . ***your way***. *There is no right or wrong way to express any feeling*, so long as it is genuinely yours.

11

Anger

(predominant and/or intermittent)

As with sadness, anger for some of us can dominate our life. Particularly among men, almost anything that goes wrong can precipitate an angry outburst. One of the drawbacks of indulging in the expression of anger is that such outbursts cause people to keep away from you. This can potentially bring up other feelings of not being understood or perhaps being rejected.

Anger management

With the advent of "Anger management classes" anger has become more accepted as a legitimate feeling, provided that its expression is not harmful. In Primal Therapy, safely expressing anger can in itself be therapeutic. If, at the onset of feeling anger, one can get on the floor and attempt to express it safely (often by thumping your fist into a pillow or cushion and permitting yourself to express expletives) the feeling can be acknowledged and released without harming anyone or damaging things. Again, as with sadness, such exercises do not necessarily yield quick insights, but the chances of seeing patterns that have persisted over time, usually come to mind spontaneously after emotional release and can be very beneficial. It will keep one from letting anger mount to a point where upon expressing anger, one just goes berserk, really smashing things, hitting people, and generally being violent.

Violence, I contend, is the buildup of unexpressed anger until it hits a stage where we feel the need to just go totally crazy (berserk). Men tend to access anger as part of their feelings more easily than females, but there are some very angry females also. The ability to lie down and strike a mattress or cushion or punch a pillow can take away some of the power of the anger. As with all these feelings, anger has its roots in early childhood, infanthood, and womb life. As I stated regarding sadness, *refrain* from trying to '*figure out*', where it comes from and when it started. Just let the feeling and its expression take you where you need to go, according to your body and not your head (thoughts and rationales). The same Alexander technique of "*let it happen*" applies equally well here.

The best situation for allowing this to happen (as with sadness) is a darkened room (closed curtains) and as few distractions as possible.

Keeping the noise level down so as not to disturb roommates and neighbors, is strongly advised, especially for raging anger. You need to attract as little attention as possible, by letting your expletives be muffled with a pillow or cushion. Neighbors hearing raging, angry outbursts are very likely to call the police or other neighbors, especially if you are doing this in the night and disturbing their sleep. Screaming your feelings can be difficult, but use your own discretion and dampen the sound, as best you can. Also, '*anger*' is not likely to be resolved in one or two sessions and may need to go on for many, many months . . . even years.

As with sadness, over time, you will begin to feel the power of the anger subside. What I mean by subsiding is that it becomes less intense and the need to smash things and blame others evaporates. It becomes a realization that your anger belongs to you and that others are merely a catalyst in precipitating the feeling . . . way out of proportion to that situation. As time progresses in expressing it, ones understanding of it (insights perhaps) render it to be expresses simply and directly . . . and not as blame. The eventual realization of this is very powerful and also very healthy, but it will take time. It took many events in your early life to create this as an act-out, and it will need persistence and patience to overcome it, rather than blame.

Also as with sadness, you will not always feel overwhelmed with *anger*, but even so, it is expedient to be on the floor, feeling and expressing it. Feeling it may not require you to be on the floor, but I suggest that you *get on the floor anyway*. Over time, you will, as I keep repeating, feel the benefits and the healthiness of feeling and expressing anger.

Anger is a natural human emotion (seemingly for many other creatures also), but once you have dealt with most of your past angers, expressing anger in the present is simple and direct and often needs little more than one or two sentences to express. Being able to express it this simply is usually a great relief.

There is one potential misconception about anger, especially anger in the present. Within the expression of anger there is often the need to expand on the reason for anger. It is in this expansion of the reason that there is often a 'blame game'. What I mean with this is that we can find ourselves talking about the person who brought on the anger and going on about them and who and what they are to us. This takes us away from the feeling and expressing it, and puts us in the mode of analyzing that person.

That is counterproductive. However, stating what that other person did that precipitated one's anger is legitimate, but going "off" about their character is the potential danger here. "Going off" this way more than likely will prevent any resolution of one's anger; since the person in question will remain the same. Our need is to get to know and feel what about them pushed us to be angry and to use simple words, such as "leave me alone", that hurt/upset me" or simply "that pissed me off". Surprisingly often, we discover a similarity between that person and a parent and discover aspects of our childhood we had forgotten, but felt deeply many years ago.

This can be difficult to grasp at first, but with practice it becomes obvious.

12

Fear

(Persistent and/or intermittent, also paranoia)

Fear is perhaps the most difficult of all the feelings to get on the floor with and express, at least for me. Also, the expression of fear can be complex and different for each of us. In my experience it can range from *crying* about it all the way to wanting to *scream,* and in some cases just *freezing up over it.* Fear, I find, is the most debilitating of the feelings and can be brought on by **panic attacks.** Most of us tend to run away as quickly as possible from *panic attacks,* but I would suggest, *if you can,* lie down with them and *let them happen.* The major reason for running away from them is they feel like death, a feeling that is extremely hard to face. When it happened to me in that London Clinic, I could **not** believe the force of the fear and was screaming at the top of my lungs, "I'm dying, I'm dying." I didn't die, in-spite of the feeling that I was dying. Only in hindsight did I realize I was **re-living** a moment in early childhood when I felt I was dying.

I hope my story helps, but I also know that it is very hard to feel otherwise. However, there are other experiences in life that are scarier than all hell, but as with sadness and anger, you need to take the very same precautions. There is one other factor that might help, and that is to have someone to sit with you while you go through your fears.

Having someone to '*sit with you,'* (be there for you), is something I will go into in a later chapter on buddying. It needs to be someone you absolutely trust who is NOT going to **play with your head before, during, or afterwards**. The trouble with having someone sit with you during a fear episode is that it is likely to *bring up that person's own fear* and that can greatly complicate matters.

However, in order to go down into the depth of fear, *a panic attack,* you need to feel a relative safety around you. Feeling safe environmentally while in a fear state seems like a contradiction, but this concept will make sense if you are able to go into these fears several times.

All this is very difficult to write about as there are so many permutations to the circumstances . . . So! **Proceed with caution!**

The feeling of fear and its expression can be complex: how do you express it? This is not something you *can figure out*. *"Letting it happen"* initially seems not to make sense, until you have gone through it. Before and during the descent into the fear can be devastating. It is little wonder that we are **not** prepared to face it. Even days after my first experience in that London clinic, I was still overwhelmed by what it all meant, even though the insights afterwards were very revealing. That is why I ask that you refrain from trying to make sense of it. Let the feeling tell you all you need to know about it . . . . *Yes, easier said than done.*

The circumstances of panic attacks, especially, *are* not things you can choose. There is a tendency for such attacks to happen willy-nilly at any time of the day and night. The same precautions should be observed about others, lest they rush to try to help and actually make matters worse. If you live with others and want to be able to *"let it happen,"* it might be a good idea to talk to those you live with and let them know what you are about to try. Well-meaning does not necessarily bring about the best circumstances, but if others know, chances are they'll accept your wishes. Again, someone undergoing a *panic attack* might set others off too. A room full of people having fear episodes is not conducive to a reasonable resolution. So, take great care if you decide to have another person *sit for you*. Give them as much preparation as possible, even letting them read this chapter, so that they know something of what to expect.

13

Other Experiences

(that are not strictly feeling)

Suicidal

The first of these and the most devastating of all is feeling suicidal. According to Janov being suicidal occurs when old feelings are on the rise; but they are so daunting that the person feels they are beyond bearable. If the feelings persist there is a tendency not to know where to turn or get help. It is beyond the purview of this book to suggest how one might deal with these feelings. In general, suicidal feelings arise when current difficulties seem insurmountable, stirring up long-repressed feelings of helplessness originally felt in infancy. For those not having felt suicidal, it is very hard to explain the devastation going on inside. It is often accompanied by feelings of hopelessness and/or helplessness. One runs around looking for hope, relief, answers, or anything rather than the deep, deep despair. It might help a little if you can begin to cry about your utter despair.

Perhaps it might be expedient to suggest some of the things that bring about the feeling of wanting to die. To die is the final "cop-out", for, it does seemingly offer respite . . . even peace. I do suggest that any person feeling suicidal should get some professional help or at least try the telephone suicide hot lines. These people usually know how to listen.

On the one occasion I was suicidal, I ran around seeking people who would just listen to me, but most were only willing to give me five minutes and then wanted out. This was devastating. Slowly, the desire to end it all did subside, but it took a long time to get there.

The immediate reasons for feeling suicidal are many: death of a loved one, rejection or even physical separation. Others could be one's inability to connect with another human being; physical handicaps brought about by war, accidents, or natural disasters; and often loneliness in old age, when all past friends are gone.

All I am able offer the suicidal-minded person is that this impulse arises from an even deeper pain, perhaps from the womb at the time of birth, or rejection from caregivers very early in life.

I realize that this may not be perceived as an adequate consolation, but understanding that part of the suicidal impulse may originate from experiences dating back to infancy can actually offer some hope. By feeling and expressing reactions to those early traumas, thus seeing them in their real context, the enormity of the pain in your present context will lessen. Again, the only suggestion I can offer, other than professional help, is to cry about one's despair. This just might be a start.

Depression

This next pseudo-feeling is also very daunting to those who suffer it. It is brought about by **sitting on top of deep pain**.

Depression is equally difficult to resolve, but I do suggest that finding ways to express real feelings of Sadness, Anger, and Fear can alleviate some of their power. It is a long process, but just feeling underlying feelings can greatly help a depressed person to cope.

The medications offered by the medical profession are helpful to many, but I have heard from some who take anti-depressants that they feel a diminished sense of the bounty of life; some have even rejected these medications. I will talk about medications in the chapter on medicine. In general, the side effects of medications are a definite *downside*. There is no '*free lunch*' as the saying goes.

For the depressive willing to try feelings and express them: follow what I have said in the previous chapters on Sadness, Anger, and Fear.

If the medications are working for you and you feel a relative contentment, then you may wish to leave feelings alone.

Violent Rage

Being consumed with violent rage is also a cover for deeper feelings, and akin to anger. The repression of anger in early childhood just gets stored in the subconscious. Later in life, these angers come to the surface and are manifested often by a sense of violent outrage. Again, a willingness to lie down and feel the outrageousness and the anger is the way to dissipate this **all consuming rage**. *Again, doing so is not easy* and doesn't follow in a straight line, but after many sessions of feeling the rage and expressing whatever one can, will lessen the power (valance) of the rage. Follow your bodily feeling and *refrain* from trying to *figure it out.*

Misery

This next one is not quite so serious, but it can be very disconcerting. To be in a near constant miserable state can make life unbearable. Like all other deeper feelings, misery is usually sitting atop other deeper feelings. One needs to lie down with the feeling and express some words that seem appropriate to the misery. Slowly, the misery will not feel as daunting and may eventually offer some great relief. *Again: easier said than done.*

Chronic Anxiety

To go through life being forever anxious is another disconcerting state of being. The problem with anxiety is that there seems no reason for it on one level, yet to the sufferer there seems no way to make it go away or to know the why and wherefore. The trouble with this condition is that it garners very little sympathy from others, who are constantly telling you that your state is unreasonable. You hear their words (*"Pull yourself together!"*), but how to do so eludes you.

The method is the same as for all other feeling: just lie down with it and say all that the feeling *seems* to want to say. Again, try not *to figure anything out;* that is counter-productive.

Confusion

This is a strange and not very common state of being, but for those suffering it, it is debilitating. The very same mechanism that *creates the other pseudo feelings* applies also here. It often goes back to a state of confusion in womb life and early childhood. The very young child is not able to figure anything out. Severe confusion can be the beginning of what we often call schizophrenia. Chronic confusion for the child not having the ability to make any sense of it may actually help create exactly this situation. Some mental health professions have deemed schizophrenia to be an organic brain disorder, but suggest little by way of the cause and when this disorder took place. Janov has suggested that unless and until we look at these aberrations of people in their historical context then we confuse the very diagnosis. I concur with that assessment.

It is very hard to resolve this condition. However, in its lesser forms it is manageable if we are prepared to lie down and feel whatever is there and express it, through words or whatever seems appropriate. As with the other states, *it does take time*. For the chronically confused it may require more than I can suggest here. The main reason for mentioning it is that it just might offer some explanation that the sufferer can take to professionals offering help.

Boredom

This particular state is very common and leaves many with few options to transcend it. Much of it can be put down to our capitalist system wherein we are forced into having to do uninspiring, just plain boring work that we hate. We need to at least be able to get a pay check at the end of the pay period. It is unbelievable how many of us tolerate this status quo. What is life about if, for the most part, we are coerced into this means to survive, through a pay check? For all that, boredom is perhaps the least painful of these '*pseudo*' feelings, as I call them. The way to transcend it is the very same as with the other states: feeling this boredom intensely and expressing vocally our resentment towards it. *All else leads from there.*

Initially, it may seem that this is not taking us very far. But after some time lying with this feeling and expressing our displeasure, there is a surprising relief eventually and the insight that we *don't have to tolerate* this boredom, at least to the extent that we do . . . becomes clearer.

Bitterness

One last one: for the moment. Bitterness is something more akin to an act-out rather than a state of being. If we persist in it, it begins to take on a life of its own and becomes a means for blame. However, the feeling of sadness is, in my opinion, a way to transcend it. Sadly: staying bitter does not work and like with all the other states, to feel what is driving this feeling and to express what is bugging us more deeply is the solution. This process requires a great deal of time to get through, **but** doing so can eventually dissipate the bitterness.

14

Buddying

(or having someone to sit with and be there for you.)

The word "buddy" was brought into prominence during WWII when soldiers in close combat became very close to one another and struck up very, very close relationships. Janov took the word and applied it to fellow patients so that there could be a very close and trusting relationship between patients undergoing the therapy. It has worked very well for me. I have had many buddies and to this day have three people that I am very close and trusting with.

Just as they sit for you, in turn you sit for them. Because each is familiar with the process and their buddy; a rapport is struck up. I am not advocating the very same principle with people getting into their feelings on their own. There are some drawbacks to buddying. The first one is that the buddy can become very suggestive to the one on the floor. Without quite a lot of experience with the therapy *there is the chance for the buddy to make very inappropriate suggestions.* It is very easy for someone outside your feelings to suggest the way **they** feel and not the way **you** ought to proceed. I want to stress that **you should totally refrain from offering such suggestions**, which can potentially be very dangerous, extremely distracting, and will likely lead the one on the floor to mistrust you.

Equally, the one on the floor may start to look for encouragement or validation for what he or she is doing. I sincerely suggest that you *refrain* from doing this also and learn to **trust your OWN feelings**. In the end, trusting your feelings is what is most important, and gaining access to those feelings in **your own way** is where I feel this process needs to go. Again: *easier said than done.*

Someone sitting for you serves best as a deflector of potential neighborly busybodies. The buddy can reassure the enquirer that all is okay. Also, it is re-assuring for anyone experiencing deep painful feelings to know simply that another person is present; to take away some of the fear and anxiety of being totally alone.

15

Intermittent Feelings

(not everyone is overwhelmed by feelings all the time)

It may be that you only occasionally feel sad or any other strong feelings. I still suggest that at the onset of these feelings you get on the floor, feel, and express them the best way you can. **Trust the process.** Doing so requires mainly that you **trust your *inner being*.** There may be times when the nature of your feelings is in doubt. This is very understandable. Just be patient with your self. Take breaks then get on the floor again when a feeling seems more accessible.

Feelings as the means to health

Feeling your feelings, as opposed to suppressing them, is what I am proposing here as the means to health. I recognize that this proposition goes completely against the general trend.

The commonly accepted view these days is that our health depends upon diet (what we eat) and exercise. I would like to take on this trend by suggesting that a feeling-full creature will naturally eat right, know exactly what exercise his or her body requires, and when to eat or exercise. A feeling-full person knows those things instinctively.

We do not require so-called "experts" in the medical field to tell us all this. ***You are the best expert about your being—if you will just trust that notion.*** Experts put us psychologically in their hands and make us believe they know better than our inner selves. ***To me the notion that others know better is the great fallacy of modern times.*** Follow your instincts and feelings. They will tell you everything about yourself (*and only about yourself*). ***We also need to refrain from being the expert to other people*** . . . and that includes our children.

This rule also applies to those tempted to "help" others who wish to get into their feelings. It is best merely say how it was/is for you, even if the other is seeking your advice about this.

The only thing we truly know is what **WE personally** feel. *And what I feel IS NOT what you feel.* All other so-called knowledge is irrelevant . . . **circumstantial evidence at best**.

In Summary

Feelings are the very core of our being, but unfortunately most of us lose access to those feelings early in life at the onset of becoming repressed (neurotic). We live our lives depriving ourselves of our feelings because we subconsciously assume they are too frightening, painful, and/or confusing to experience, especially after a lifetime of neglect. We need to get back to feelings. I readily admit that this concept is completely new and radically unlike the way we humans have tried to solve our problems for eons. This is precisely why I say: *The discovery of Primal Pain is the greatest discovery mankind ever made* . . . or for that matter . . . *will ever make.* It's about our very being . . . our **real nature**.

16

Withdrawal

(withdrawing from addictions)

Any attempt to get into your feelings and get results requires that you quit all behaviors that kill pain. For someone attempting to totally withdraw from *all* painkilling behaviors and ingestions immediately could be mighty difficult. If you have such habits, then it would probably be expedient to just take those that seem the most prominent . . . those that you habitually go for to feel better when feelings come up. Smoking and drinking are perhaps the most common. Giving these up "cold turkey" is not necessarily the best idea. So, maybe it would be smart to try to cut down on some of the more obvious ones. For serious addictions that are dangerous to your well-being, you should make a concerted effort to eliminate or cut back on these. The first thing to be aware of in quitting any addiction is that it will be replaced by upcoming pain. We tend to think that quitting means depriving ourselves of some assumed pleasure or ingredient necessary to our survival. This assumption is part of the denial of reality associated with addictive practices.

Pain, and your attempt to suppress it, is the driving force, although your mind may go through several contortions to try to see it otherwise. Each of our addictions has a history. One that I am aware of is the over-eating addiction. It might be helpful for over-eaters to spend some time simply contemplating the fact that the amount we ingest is not totally necessary to survival, although it may seem as if it is. Similarly, people who smoke may feel that quitting takes away all the joy of life, but there was a time in our lives when we were very young and did not smoke and we didn't die of boredom then. The same applies to not drinking (alcohol) which to the alcoholic at first may seem like taking away the joy of living. Again, we did not always drink and we did survive. The same dynamic would apply to gambling and sex addictions. I used to rationalize that sex was a natural part of life and that without my 'hunt' there would be no point to my existence.

What else should I occupy my time with? Gambling offers the chance to get rich with seemingly little effort. If only we could predict the winner. Another is overworking to keep oneself occupied. This one could be rationalized as making oneself useful in the workplace or in one's business. Again, **it is all a means of killing pain.**

Twelve-Step Programs

Quitting any of these will bring up pain and if we are just able to lie down with the feeling and cry or sob for what we seemingly had to give up, eventually the compulsion will diminish. However, if you try to give up too much at once you could find yourself overwhelmed. **I do not recommend that.** Take the compulsion that is most dangerous to you and work on that one first. There are many twelve-step programs for most of these compulsions. They might be very helpful, especially if you know from the get-go that once you give them up the pain will rise, even though you may suggest to yourself that it was not rising pain.

The twelve step programs were first thought through by two alcoholics who pondered the reason for their addiction. I personally do not fully agree with their initial premise, but do acknowledge that for many it has proved to be the only means to quit. If we can accept the pain-killing factor of our addictions, that is a great psychological advantage.

There is little else to consider when contemplating withdrawal from these compulsions/addictions, except to go into a listing of the ones I am able to think of:

Ingestions:
    Alcoholism,
    Nicotine,
    Over-eating,
    Mood enhancing/pain suppressing drugs, both legal and illegal.

Behaviors:
    Overworking or "workaholism" (addiction),
    Gambling (something for nothing)
    Sex-addiction (the thrill)

17

Medicine

(trying to cure the incurable)

I am going to stick my neck out here and state that the medical profession is extremely remiss in not seriously considering Primal Theory. I am not sure of the overall reasoning, but I suspect that they did not want to recognize the validity and importance of a discovery by a psychologist. Had Janov been a psychiatrist (an MD), they might have looked at the discovery more closely. Further, the fact that Janov was resistant to describing the methodology of his therapy made the medical establishment even more reluctant to accept the therapy's value. Also, current medical professional standards require that therapy types undergo peer review. This Janov was not willing to do either, IMO.

What is the Medical Profession?

Not too long ago people went to the barber shop to get the standard remedy for many health conditions: blood letting. We've progressed from there to taking herbs and brews that might alleviate many of those same conditions. Much of this was somewhat more natural and effective. What we have now is a chemical industry, termed pharmacology, eager to make profit in our capitalist system through modern refinements of the old herbal remedies, isolating the essential ingredients of those herbs that tend to alleviate specific ailments, and in many cases making them easier to ingest. Another route the medical profession has pursued is to delve into the microbiology of our bodies in hopes of figuring out precisely how these chemicals and herbal ingredients work. It might seem natural and normal to continue this endless pursuit, but the profession has refused to wonder if it might be going off on a tangent. The holistic medicines tried to rectify some of these notions without much success, sort of going down Lewis Carroll's rabbit hole.

The major current culprit is the neurophysiology profession, especially, with the advent of MRI (Magnetic Resonance Imaging) and so-called readings of brain physiology.

Hold on: maybe we should backtrack a little!

Now here's me coming from the notion of Primal Theory, suggesting that **real health** is our ability to feel. My notion that neurosis is our one disease and that all other diseases, ailments, and discomforts are mere symptoms of this one disease, will infuriate the medical, pharmacological, and micro biology professions. These professions are making it ever more complex and expensive to offer health-care on any great scale. Left-wing politics suggests a more compassionate approach. Right-wing politics, having little by way of compassion, offers only capitalist (business) ways to solve the problem from a corporate standpoint. To me, both are going down the Lewis Carroll's rabbit hole. That's why I suggest, "hold on, let's backtrack a little."

Reverberation of Unexpressed Feelings

Janov suggested that feelings that fail to get expressed and get stored in what I call the subconscious, reverberate in the body, spending a lifetime, looking for an outlet to express themselves. These reverberations, as he called them (which I feel is a great description of what is taking place), continue for decades, eventually causing a malfunction of the body organs. These malfunctions occur in the weakest part of our physiology. They manifest themselves in what we call "diseases" (usually of older people), like cancer, Alzheimer's, Parkinson's, Hodgkin's, Lou Gehrig, etc. It requires a very good understanding of Primal Theory to grasp this. I contend that, unless and until **the health care professions** come to terms with this holistic view, we will forever be looking to pharmacology and microbiology to find the cause; then attempt to cure the symptoms without getting to the very sources (history) of the problem. Sadly, I fear that my words here will fall on 'deaf ears' in the health-care professions . . . *until who knows when . . . if ever . . . alas.*

Where do we go from here?

So, where do we go from here? What I am going to say next is most controversial of all. Janov has been suggesting for some time now that the only recourse we have is to **feel** our way to health is via (through) his therapy. My point is that there are never going to be enough therapists to give every one Primal Therapy. So other than a 'do-it-yourself' feeling guide there is little else we can do. I am going to suggest one other avenue, but that avenue might create even more controversy than I bargain for.

Mood Elevating Drugs

The mood elevating drugs other than those offered by the medical profession are the pain killers Heroin, Opium, Cocaine, Methamphetamines ("Speed"), and Ecstasy. The **king** of the pain killers is heroin. This has been made illegal by all nations based on its addictiveness, yet most of the prescribed pharmaceuticals are also addictive. What is stupid about all this is that one way or another we are all addicted to either ingesting something (alcohol and nicotine being the most common) or a behavior (overeating, sex, gambling etc.) so why should addiction to heroin or opium be any less harmful? It is a relatively easy and cheap drug and if as Janov postulates it is the pain from the past that causes most diseases/disorders of later life. If Primal Theory was intelligently understood: it suggests IMO that if we can kill 'Primal Pain' even with a very addictive drug . . . this could facilitate the enormous costs of the health care system. Of course, there are some minor complications I hope to go into later.

Two reasons heroin might be considered outrageous and dangerous are that: 1) the only way to administer is with needles. I am not sure that there is a possibility to administer this drug any other way, but it might be worth investigating. 2) The other reason is the proclivity to OVERDOSE (OD). I contend the reason is that the heroin addict attempts to recapture that initial euphoria when they first used it. I suggest that anyone using heroin as a pain-killer MUST understand that, that initial euphoria is not possible to recapture, without risking the tendency to overdose . . . and die in the process. The proclivity to recapture that initial euphoria . . . and method of ingestion . . . might be worth investigating.

More Recent Reasoning's About Drug Taking: "The War on Drugs"

There has been a debate about illegal drugs and the ramifications of drug remedy, and the violent "drug cartels." It is worth considering an effective and relatively cheap health-care remedy for many of the diseases, especially in later life. One example might be that heroin could be a remedy/cure for cancer. It is worth experimenting with (controversial I do know). This is another of my notions about prohibiting drug use. Preconceived notions and the "War on Drugs" may need to be re-thought and perhaps discarded.

The Feeling Enhancing Drugs

Another class of mood elevating drugs is the feeling enhancement drugs, the most common being; Marijuana (Cannabis), Lysergic Acid (LSD) and mushrooms (psilocybin). Why these are deemed dangerous has never been fully discussed or studied. If these drugs are able to facilitate feelings, it could be a way to help with a feeling therapy. *The real danger here* is that one might descend into a feeling that the person is not ready to feel, let alone express. Certainly the more drastic LSD should be refrained from *until one is very, Very, VERY familiar with their feelings.*

As Janov has stated repeatedly, these drugs can precipitate going into feelings out-of-sequence and cause more problems rather than they resolve. More recently it has been acknowledged that cannabis (marijuana) can help with diseases. I certainly suggest the reasoning here is that the very diseases in question are an '*act-in*' against feeling-full-ness. If this is correct, then it is obvious that to become more feeling-full through the use of these feeling-enhancing drugs will naturally be a means of relieving the effects of these act-ins (diseases). I believe these ideas are worthy of consideration and experiments, especially if the experimenters were to familiarize themselves with Primal Theory. Maybe I am asking too much too quickly; BUT, my feeling is, we do not have a great deal of time left if we carry on with this debilitating disease: neurosis.

With both of these classes of drugs there ought to be more thought and research to see if they might be helpful. Those suffering grievously from Primal pain need to get beyond the utter craziness of alcohol and nicotine as pain-killing drugs. Alcohol is slowly killing those ingesting it and the social harm from alcohol and nicotine as accepted drugs is now being realized. It is quite obvious why alcohol was a prohibited in the 1920's. The reason for rescinding prohibition was because alcohol was such a popular and easily available pain-killer. I am not sure what the repercussions of this discussion will be, BUT it is one that needs some extensive debate, if we are able to get beyond biases and preconceived notions. What is obvious is that individuals in grievous pain need help. Those willing to use drugs need to understand what they are doing and what is involved.

This chapter is my attempt to take on the preconceived notions of **real health.** We need to re-think many notions that have become embedded into our present cultures and habits. The very nature of **real health** is beyond the scope of current medical science, even though Janov spent a great deal of effort discussing how the practice of Primal Therapy fits into it. In a nut-shell, the real human being **was initially a feeling-full creature,** BUT all we are left to study now is the non-feeling creature . . . the neurotic human.

This takes us down Lewis Carroll's rabbit hole and into an ever-decreasing list of reasons for the very existence of disease. I reiterate: *I am claiming that there is only one disease and that all other so-called 'diseases' are merely symptoms of that one disease.* This will be a very hard sell to those who believe in our current notion of medicine.

If you are willing to contemplate much of what I have suggested here, a very simple notion of getting back to our *feeling-full-ness,* you are beginning to see that the therapy I have been describing, in this short book has the potential of moving humans toward *real health* in a very cheap and easy manner, without complex pharmacology and microbiology. Of course, it is not a simple straightforward process because of the decades most of us have spent in the current medical environment.

Primal Theory: Its Study and at Least a Willingness to Accept it.

I spent the first part of this book writing about this theory. For this chapter, I am going to ask you, the reader, to accept my prognosis (based on Primal Theory) of why **real health** is to be found in *feeling-full-ness*, which is, in essence, where Primal therapy aims to take its patients.

We are born feeling and everything stems from this one premise. We learn everything until such a time as we have some notion of what operating mode our caregivers are attempting to push and manipulate us into adopting . . . most of which we actually attempt to rebel against. The ferocity of the caregivers' manipulations affects how weakly or strongly we resist. Our learning process, if left to our own natural inclinations, would leave our natural talents and instincts intact. Alas, this process is invariably perverted. We start down the road of perverting the **natural healthy process** that we would have instinctively followed with healthy caregivers. **It is a slow and a not obvious perversion of our health**, but I hope I have demonstrated that this is the beginning of all our subsequent illnesses, diseases, and later drastic ailments such as depression, Cancer, Alzheimer's, Lou-Gehrig's, Parkinson's, Hodgkin's and all the other strange diseases.

The Efficacy of Primal Therapy

It is because of this very notion that Primal Therapy works. This book is written for those that have some awareness of the potential of Primal Therapy, but are unable, for any number of reasons, to get access to do the therapy.

I repeat, you will not get Primal therapy, but you could get to a place of **greater health** by just permitting yourself to feel. Learning to feel is a simple notion, but actually doing so is a difficult and sometimes demanding practice that is always extremely rewarding.

Youthful Rebelliousness

I feel that the rebelliousness of youth in puberty is a deep subliminal sensation. We are leaving our childhood, where we were given, in many cases, at least some ability to feel and express many feelings, especially sadness by crying. Now on entering adulthood, we are not given that license and are bombarded with admonitions to be "***grown-up***" and be an adult. Reading this book—a great deal of this you can apply to yourself and see perhaps how things got all screwed up in your own upbringing. This is not meant to be a **blame game**, but rather a means to hopefully rectify some of the damage. Nor is it about ***forgiveness either***, which I find counter productive, because of the ferocity and depth of this damage that makes getting into your own feeling very daunting. It does not matter whether or not, you are able to delve into the depth of your history, but that you are able, on an on-going basis, to get deeper and deeper into your own feelings and an ability to **express** those feelings. This is your fundamental nature: just being able to simply and freely re-learn to let your feelings happen and express them, as best you can, in your own good way, *and* in your own good time, is the ***Royal Road to health***.

Having a feeling

There is as notion, I feel, that having a feeling is all that is required. I want to emphasize that just feeling a feeling is only half of the FULL FEELING. It needs to be ***expressed***. Feeling the sensation and expressing it fully is the key. Some claim that merely talking about feelings is the very same as expressing them. To me, even though in many cases talking about a feeling may be the only way to begin to feel the feeling, these feelings are not fully expressed by words alone, but through a physical release such as crying or pounding a pillow.

18

Psychology

(why we think and behave the way we do)

The great schism in the psychological community regarding Primal Therapy versus cognitive and/or behavioral therapies has not prompted an adequate debate about the differences between the two. As I see it, the former is subjective and the latter is objective. Even if we are being asked about ourselves, and our past experiences. We are being asked to be reflective. In the cognitive therapies we become aware of events in the past, but are merely asked to note that awareness, or worse, to *think* about past events. Primal therapy is about experiencing a *feeling* related to that event and expressing the feeling, not an *awareness or thought* about it. Herein is a whole new way of experiencing therapy. Exploring the *expression of feeling* is the therapeutic paradigm. However, as stated earlier in this book, **no-one has a monopoly on feelings**. Feelings are something we all know within our being, even if only to the extent that I know I itch somewhere. Children are very aware of feelings and are close to them almost all the time.

Feeling Therapy and Primal Therapy

I want to convey to the reader both the similarity of Primal Therapy to Feeling therapy and the distinction between the two. Primal Therapy is the domain of the Primal Institute and the Primal Center. A 'do-it-yourself feeling therapy' is different in the sense that a therapist, with extensive experience helping to guide the patient towards the feeling experience is NOT available to the *do-it-yourselfer*. Conceptually, doing a feeling therapy on your own requires that you need to **trust your feelings** and **instincts** you come to: The reason for doing it on your own in the first place.

We need to re-think therapy; it is for this reason that I put the emphasis on **health** and not **therapy**. Further, I feel the need to get

Jack Waddington

away from the subject of psychology: the study of the mind. Getting into feelings and some of the daunting sensations that we are likely to encounter should allow us to **think of Feeling Therapy in terms of living healthfully** and **not some objective process.**

19

Warning

(especially to the casual reader)

I offered a warning at the very beginning of this book and I wish here to repeat that warning. There is a sense, especially here in the United States, that if you try something and it doesn't work for you, then **sue for some recompense.** This is precisely why I wish to repeat this warning:

Someone attempting to get into feelings on their own, then discovering that the process is getting scary and is not providing improvement as quickly as they had hoped, might try to use this experience as a means for demanding compensation with the help of clever, unscrupulous lawyers. This type of person is looking for a quick fix. *There isn't a quick fix!*

ANYONE feeling overwhelmed or; that the therapy is not working should simply revert back to all those ways (ingestions and behaviors) you were involved with before you read this book. They were, by definition, what you depended on in living your life up until that point, and in fact they **were effective** for you at that time. Reverting back to them is the simplest and most effective way to relieve yourself from any assumed detrimental affect of your attempt to FEEL.

It is for this reason that this book is for those who have some understanding (cognizance) of Primal Therapy and Primal Theory and are willing to do feeling therapy with the aim of becoming a healthier human being. These people might have been wondering for years how they might benefit from Primal Therapy if they were able to do so.

I again repeat, you will not be doing Primal Therapy . . . that is the domain of The Primal Institute or the Primal Center, both here in Los Angeles County. Instead, you will be doing Feeling Therapy which has many of the same benefits if pursued with courage and patience.

However, I repeat: no-one has a monopoly on feelings and almost all of us were born feeling-full. To quote a phrase . . . feelings are your "God-given right" OR better still: '**your birthright.**'

20

Belief and Faith in Feelings

Belief is a noun which in essence means you don't know. That is why I added the word faith here, meaning that you must have enough faith in yourself to know deep down there is correctness to the suggestion of this book that all you need is access to your feelings to improve your health. It is yet another neurotic notion that science (a product of egotistic, thinking humans) is capable of yielding the same results.

There is an Internet article from London by Aubrey de Grey, a biomedical gerontologist, entitled "Who wants to live forever? Scientist sees aging cured," He states that the first person to reach the age of 150 is already born and that there is a possibility through biomedical gerontology that within 20 years a person could expect to live to be 1,000 years old. This biomedical gerontologist is of the mindset that the biomedical world is capable of creating such longevity . . . based on what? He does not say.

To me, such notions stretch the credibility of what constitutes being human. We are either a feeling-full, holistic creature or a perverted one; the perversion being neurosis (the pathology of feeling). I would stress that this belief in **thinking and science** is no more credible than that fantastic wonderland outlined by Lewis Carroll, with Mad-hatters and Queens-of-Hearts.

Just because someone or some institution has designated someone to be a biomedical gerontologist does not mean we have solved the "Theory of Everything." I have suggested that "Unified Field Theory" OR "The Theory of Everything" was defined when Arthur Janov formulated Primal Theory. My reasoning is that prior to Primal Theory we humans were floundering with our thinking brains to such an extent that our conceited ego believes us to be superior to all other creatures. I refute that notion on the simple premise that we are the only creature on the planet that attempts **to control nature** rather than to **live with it**.

Rather than getting some human to live to be 1,000 years old we had better do something very drastic in our thinking (health process) or we are going to be lucky if there will be any life left at the end of this century. Someone, for some silly notion, will start blowing up other cultures in the hope they will be the only ones to survive. The idea is already out there.

Part of our madness is searching the heavens for what is deemed "intelligent life." Our notion of intelligent life is another neurotic creature on another planet out there in outer space that is as crazy (neurotic) as we are. "Intelligence" is our own idea of who we are, without acknowledging that we are neurotic (crazy). Hence, I needed to add this chapter to demonstrate that we are "off to the races" about all-sorts of crazy (neurotic) notions.

21

Thinking

(At what point in our evolution did we start to think)

In my previous book I devoted a chapter to "The Nature of Thinking." I extrapolated this from Benjamin Lee Whorf's notion that we think in language, which he formulated in the 1940's. I made a concerted effort to see if there was any evidence that we could 'think' outside of language. I came up with a blank.

Many have refuted Whorf's postulation, but I find all those that do, argue thus from very flimsy notions. From that idea I then asked: "what did we do before language and when in our evolution did we develop language and why?" I took the notion of an anthropologist from Cambridge University, England, that mankind migrated to the colder climate of Europe from Africa, and because of the colder climate was impelled to live communally in caves. This created the necessity for these early cave dwellers to repress crying babies, for the sake of the community as a whole, and started us on the downward slope of neurosis. If Whorf's postulation is correct, then before language all we were able to do was feel as is the case with all other creatures. Therefore, I postulated that "thinking" was a perversity of our brain physiology. Ever since human cerebrums developed to a certain size, we began to believe that we are superior to other animals because of this faculty. **I refute that notion**. We are, as I previously stated, an inferior creature in that we suffer a very debilitating disease . . . neurosis.

Thinking is, by my reckoning, alien to our true being as a once feeling-full creature and my notion is that humans are a very unhealthy species considering all our ailments, diseases, disorders, and discomforts especially later in life. It requires a conceptual leap to grasp this, a leap which I find most of us are reluctant to perform. We have been, for far too long, assuming this notion of superiority because of our ability to "**think.**" I contend that most of this thinking is mankind's first act-out. I also contend that our ability to think will destroy us, nature, and the planet before this century is out, unless we learn to get back to our original state of being: creatures . . . who feel.

The Politics of Feelings

The politics of feeling is something we are not that ready to talk about. We have assumed that feelings are something beyond discussion. Further, we assume that emotions and feelings are synonymous, i.e. one and the same thing. According to Janov and myself, that is not so. A feeling is a psycho-physical event and emotion is the expression of that event. (See footnote on page 68 of "The Primal Scream.") In the opening chapters on Primal Theory I gave the example of a pin prick being a psycho-physical event, and the expression (emotion) of that event is "ouch!"

Understanding these two aspects of a full feeling event is crucial.

PART III

TRANSFORMATION

Both the next Chapter "Child-rearing" and the Epilogue are in my first book, but I repeat them here for some who might find the following views on childrearing a useful beginner's guide. The epilogue is about me. I state it in Part III for convenience. So here goes!

22

Childrearing

(merely a suggestion for a non-neurotic world)

In order to transition from our current neurotic state, we need to completely rethink our current childrearing practices. Therefore, to me, this is a very important chapter. However, I hesitate a lot to even make any suggestion here since I have never brought a child into this world, let alone reared one. My only authority is that I was once a child, so this is from a child's perspective, not a parent's. Since I do not know any parent who succeeded in rearing a non-neurotic child, I feel that parental experience counts for very little. It could be said that I have no ideas about the difficulties, but I contend that 99% of the difficulties with childrearing are due to traumatizing the child (inadvertently perhaps) and not the upbringing, per se.

We need to accept that children, even newborns, are sovereign unto themselves. The child's fully feeling self will respond appropriately to get its needs met and a fully feeling parent will know instinctively what the child needs. As the child progresses in life, it will become easier and easier on parents to just allow the child to decide what it needs and wants. To understand the difference between *need* and *want*, however, necessitates fully feeling parents.

What could be done to let the child be itself when the parent is still neurotic? This is a question that many who have done Primal Therapy for an extended period of time find difficult to answer. There is no "how to" that I can tell anyone, nor is there anyone I know of who can give a "how to." I will proffer one suggestion—as best you can, attempt at all times (especially in the first year) to stay with the child, holding it, and sense what the child is asking for by using your own feelings.

There are several books that I feel would be helpful. The first relates to the very birthing process: *Birth Without Violence* by Dr. Frederick LeBoyer, a French obstetrician. Another is *The Continuum Concept* by

Jean Leidloff who studied childrearing practices among the indigenous tribes of the Andes.

Also, there is a book by a father who brought up his own son after he divorced: *Real Fatherhood* by Bob Kamm. I cried reading this book, seeing that his child, Benjamin (affectionately called Bengi-boo) got much of what I wanted, but never fully got. Then there is an Australian documentary about some experiments with newborns called *Kangaroo Mother Care*. Each of these suggests new ways of taking care of our young and the way we might look at childrearing. Lastly, we need to look seriously into circumcision of male babies (a barbaric act if ever there was one) and caesarian section birthing.

Crying Babies

I suggest that a crying baby is a baby in pain, period. If the child is crying, it needs to be held until the caregiver (mother) can ascertain what it is that the child **needs.** There are very few possibilities after all other needs have been met. Needing to **breathe freely**, needing to be **fed**, needing to be **cleaned**, needing to be **kept warm**, needing to **feel safe**, and needing to be **held**. I contend that any mother having gone through nine months of pregnancy has many instinctive abilities to feel what the child needs. As the child develops, assuming that all prior needs are met, it becomes relatively easy for the caregivers to know what is required. By the time the child has words, gestures and can move, I contend knowing what the child needs becomes easier and easier to ascertain. The one major requisite is that the caregivers (parents) love and want that child from the outset.

If the mother is the primary caregiver, then the father **needs to be totally supportive of that mother and child** without expecting anything in return for his effort. Mothering is a total encompassing task and leaves little or no time for those two from the minute there was a child on the way. We need to dispel the myth that creating a child enhances the 'twosome' nature of the original relationship. It becomes, by definition, a 'threesome' at least. In our current neurotic world, it takes 26 hours a day for both partners to bring up just one child. Yes, that means it can never be fully achieved in our current civilization.

It is on these grounds that, if the mother (or couple) did not want the child, an abortion ought **always** to be allowable. Being unwanted creates a trauma to the fetus that continues well after birth. If the newborn is fostered off or adopted, it creates further trauma and the beginnings of neurosis, which even the most skilled and aware caregiver would find almost impossible to negate or reverse.

The Prerequisite

The prerequisite for having a child ought to be that both partners (potential parents) want that child for its own sake. Sadly, there are many reasons couples and individuals cite for wanting and having a child other than what I just stated. The egotistical one of desiring to reproduce ourselves is perhaps the worst, based on the false notion that it is a natural desire. Much of this is promoted through religious notions. Another is the common belief that having a child will enhance the relationship. Chances are greater it will do the opposite or at least make the relationship more difficult. A twosome's relationship at the onset of pregnancy becomes (I repeat) immediately a threesome (presuming that there was no other child so far). Twosomes are complicated enough without the added complication of a third human being. Further additions will complicate matters even more.

However, if both parents really want a child or children for their own sake, then they give them a great start in life. If one or the other partner does not want the child, then going ahead with the pregnancy is invariably catastrophic for that child and potentially for the relationship as well. It is suggested that abortion is killing. I agree in principle, but there is killing and killing. Sadly, we are left with the legacy of "Thou shalt not kill." Is killing a pesky fly or accidentally walking on, and killing some colony of ants crossing our path considered a sin in the eyes of God? Are a few thousands cells in a uterus any more sacrosanct than a colony of ants or a pesky fly? It appears hypocritical to me that killing a fully-grown human in war, or through the criminal justice system, seems not to cause much of a stir, yet paradoxically anti-abortionists insist on saving a few thousand cells in the uterus, based *presumably*, on the same God-given commandment.

Birth Without Violence

Dr. Frederick LeBoyer in his book *Birth Without Violence* suggested that current obstetric practices are, in many instances, violent. Since his publication, there seems to have been some movement towards making the birthing process less painful for the child. There have been studies done to show that this does indeed benefit the child in its later development, which should be obvious. There have been several other publications also pointing this out, but these are too numerous for me to recount here. Janov points this out in great detail in all of his books, particularly his latest, *Life Before Birth*. I suggest reading Janov will further elaborate on this.

Kangaroo Mother Care

Some months ago the Primal Institute showed a recorded documentary from an Australian television company, *Kangaroo Mother Care,* which moved me. It was attempting to demonstrate that, maybe, we humans as upright beings actually produced a situation in the gestation process whereby the fetus needed to be born before completion of gestation. The fact that most other creatures are able to stand within minutes of their birth may corroborate the correctness of this notion. Human babies are unable to do this and it takes a year after birth just to walk. The exception in another creature is the marsupial that has this very convenient pouch for the young to climb into after birth to stay and be nurtured with little extra attention from the mother. The program showed how some obstetricians in Australia experimented with newborns, letting them seek the breasts of the mother and from thereon being physically carried by the mother in what they cited as an extension of the gestation period. This offered the newborns the safety of being next to the mother's skin for an extended period of another 9 months. The babies were easily fed and kept warm and could reach the breast at the time they (the babies) needed to be fed. Also, the mother became acutely aware of when her offspring needed to defecate and be cleaned. It also suggested that the mother and child needed to sleep together for at least this extended gestation. We don't have the natural pouch, but it is a very easy matter to have a sling around the mother's neck and side to facilitate the carrying. It further suggested that perambulators for babies are NOT the way to go. Babies feel safer when they are in physical contact with the mother. I remember this well as a baby myself. It was unbelievable how **safe I felt** next to my "mammy", and how scary it was when not in physical contact.

Circumcision

Only neurotics could think up a practice as barbaric and stupefying unnatural as removing the foreskin of males' penises. To suggest it is cleaner and easier to manage in childhood and adulthood is absurd. I know from my younger days with other boys that the only ones that had difficulty with their penises were the ones that were never allowed to play with their own. Boys playing with their penises and pulling the foreskin back is natural and normal. It is neurotic parents that inculcate a "no-no" into their children playing with their genitals. Cultural traditions in this regard demonstrate the absurdity. Where the religious practice really originated is hard to ascertain.

Caesarian Section

Initially this was a practice reserved only for emergencies when the mother or child's life was threatened by a normal birth. Now it seems three other factors have crept into play: first, doctors' concerns about a malpractice suit unless they perform a caesarian birth rather than risk a difficult outcome; second, the greater convenience for the obstetricians' working hours; third, some mothers may be concerned about stretching the vagina. This unnatural surgery has an enormous impact on the "**to-be-born.**" Several primal patients, reliving their own caesarian birth, have noted that it leaves them with a sense of never completing. I contend further that a woman who underwent a caesarian birth herself must be unprepared to deal with birthing her own child. This practice should never be undertaken except in the most 'extreme' circumstances.

Boundaries

On the question of creating boundaries for children, I contend this is another of our neurotic, tragic myths. If parents can respond to the actions and reactions of a child through their own emotional responses (without threatening the child in any way), the child will readily accept and accommodate instinctively towards the parental emotions (expressions). Just as the child needs the freedom to express itself, so do the caregivers need to express their own feelings *appropriately* also. The child is born into an environment of caregivers (normally mother and father). If this is a fully-feeling environment, nothing more would ever be needed. If the child's needs are met, then its desires and wants will naturally be adaptable and there is no need to create "boundaries." The child will adapt to the feelings of its environment naturally: (I am not talking here of preventing danger, but even in this regard; reacting to the parents' feelings is the aim. See *Continuum Concept* by Jean Liedloff. All this is *easier said than done*, in particular if the caregiver is neurotic. Neurotics operate from act-outs and non-feeling-full responses that *always* confuse the child.

I am certain that if the caregiver responds *appropriately* to his or her own feelings, the child will accept this. When I say appropriate responses, I mean ones that are expressed directly and not as a threat or demand upon the child. This is tricky to actually describe, but in a primal context, I feel, makes a lot of sense. I will try in the next paragraph to give some examples, but these too must not be taken literally, but in their context, and the reader needs to think this through. Thinking out a game plan for boundaries is crazy. It needs to come from one's instincts and feelings, not principles. Neurotics think and act in terms of principles; sadly, they have little or no other means.

Delineating the Appropriate Feeling Responses to Children

Guidelines are easy to give, but are almost impossible to carry out. Nevertheless, I will state them. If the caregiver will express her feelings about what it is the child is doing without physically threatening or hurting the child (without *dumping* on the child), the child will be able to feel that response and, I contend, accept it without being in any way traumatized, by having to repress pain. As I stated earlier, frustrations to a child are not traumatic or harmful: the child can easily adjust to them. Trauma comes from *overwhelming feelings* that the child is unable to integrate into itself. The child is naturally feeling-full, provided that all prior needs have been met. The catch phrase is *"all prior needs have been met."* If not, then we are already on a very difficult path in rearing the child and hoping to save it from neurosis. Even so, the fewer traumas, especially in the early part of life—first year—the less acting out will be needed by that child as it develops.

Old Pain in Babies

There is one other factor that I feel is not even vaguely understood by childrearing practitioners, the medical profession or caregivers: we (as organisms) are forever attempting to bring the subconscious back into consciousness—**healing ourselves**. This starts to take place at the onset of feelings that are relegated into the subconscious. I contend that this occurs in babies and children that have already been traumatized and continues throughout life. This means that **if** the child has enough sense of safety, it **will** self-primal, i.e. relive the older trauma. For caregivers, this must be very confusing as it seems there is absolutely no reason why the child is in pain (usually crying or screaming). If this were understood, it would require that the caregiver stay with the child, holding it and **giving it a sense of safety** while it was reliving its old pain and the caregivers allowing it to happen. This might be a reoccurring event for the child, until it was able to totally integrate that trauma. Only caregivers aware of the nature of *reliving old pain* (primaling) might be sensitive enough to allow this.

It would take more than just one book to go into childrearing in light of Primal Theory. Therefore, even though I feel this chapter is the most important one for establishing a non-neurotic society, by necessity this book can only skirt this huge subject. I hope it might serve as an inspiration for others using Primal Theory. I feel going into parenting should be no more than wanting that child for the *child's* sake—**and not any other sake**—with both parents prepared to give themselves totally to the child's needs (not wants). The necessity to read many books about parenting can exacerbate the situation rather than enlighten prospective parents, even though I have suggested a few titles.

Epilogue

Primal Therapy will not save humanity or the planet. Primal Theory just might. Primal Theory is simple and easily understood. It explains all the factors about us humans that I have attempted to expound in this book. If, as I have suggested, Primal Theory is Unified Field Theory, then it surely does fall into that category of being simple and universally understandable.

If only it were possible to prevent the pain and suffering in the children of tomorrow.

I end this work relating my own progress in therapy over these 30 years. Before I do I would like to explain a few things about myself and my (neurotic) reasons for writing this book in the first place. When I first read *The Primal Scream*, I was so stricken with the book that I re-read it immediately, just to make sure that I had "gotten" it right. I was at the time living in Ibiza, one of the Balearic Islands in the Mediterranean, with lots of other hippies. It was the Haight-Ashbury of Europe. I immediately tried to win over all my hippy friends and was devastated to discover that none were interested. Maybe it had to do with me and the way I was presenting it. In hindsight, I now know that unless one is near to some devastating old feelings *The Primal Scream* seems somewhat dramatic in its claim. My need to proselytize was my neurotic desire to be heard (an old pain of mine from childhood). I was not deterred and eventually was able to save enough to come to the United States in 1981 and started therapy soon thereafter.

My Therapy

Feeling is an ongoing process and I have no doubt that I will have to continue to feel my old feelings, going deeper and deeper into my history, which suggests that I am far from cured or non-neurotic. I do feel that I have, over the years, gained greater access to my feelings and hence feel in better health.

Actually, without knowing it, I started therapy in that clinic in London. I knew after reading *The Primal Scream* that I wanted to do this therapy, not that I needed it. I was able early on to get into feelings of sadness about my childhood. It was not until later that I was able to get to some anger about what my father had done to me and my need for him. My therapy went quite well and I got into feelings very early relating mainly to my very strict father. After 18 months, I withdrew from formal therapy and worked with several buddies (fellow patients who "sit" for one another and listen in turn to one another). Then, some 5 years later, I was able to afford the yearly retreat that the Primal Institute ran each summer. I was really thrilled with the process at the retreats. An almost week-long residence program with 3-hour-long group sessions every day and other programs designed to promote feelings in a very beautiful setting, mainly in Montecito, Santa Barbara, California. I attended nearly all retreats from then on, finding it very conducive to getting into my deeper feelings. I did decide some 4 years later to start to attend group sessions again. Whenever I encountered a painful event in my life, I would go and get some private sessions with a therapist, all at the Primal Institute. Meanwhile, I was buddying with my buddies (I currently have 3) and progressing to earlier feelings in my childhood. I have had one primal about my birth and several feelings that have taken me back into the womb.

My life now feels relatively simple and I find I am able to listen, something I was hardly able to do before therapy. I am not nearly so nervous about many things and a lot of my twitching and neck twisting seems to have relaxed. I see other people's primal pain more easily, which allows me to be more sympathetic towards them and reduces my potential to be upset with the personalities of others. Also, I see more clearly the reason for most things and hence feel less confused. The greatest attribute is: life is way more magical and way, way less mysterious. Another benefit is knowing why I am the way I am: the "good," the "bad," and the downright "ugly." One last point: my experience fulfilled the promise Arthur Janov made in *The Primal Scream* that Primal Therapy can help us become our real selves. Indeed, I have become much closer to being the real me.

───────────

Primal Theory is very simple and easy to understand and learn, even by children who are closer to feelings and instincts. It explains all the factors about us humans, as I have attempted to explain in this book. The ramifications (implications) would help us humans create a new course for life and living. The fact that it did not catch on initially was a surprise to me, but viewing the psychological profession and knowing the neurosis of mankind, it is not surprising that the profession claims Primal Theory is too simplistic. The healthcare professionals are too vested in their complicated and sophisticated current system to give all that up. Stephen Hawking, in his book *A Brief History of Time*, suggests that when and if we discover Unified Field Theory, it would need to be simple and understandable by all of us and not just sophisticated physicists and mathematicians. If, as I have suggested, Primal Theory is Unified Field Theory, then it surely does fall into that category of being simple and universally understandable. The nature of the thinking mind is only part of the fully-feeling process and all creatures, including ourselves, are creatures of feelings. Alas, we have repressed almost all of our feelings.

———

I would like to summarize what I have written here and explain as best I can what Primal Therapy is about. Primal Therapy is a therapy to *feel what feeling feelings feels like*. That may sound convoluted, but it is a complicated process. Primal Theory is very simple, the practice of Primal Therapy is quite complex and can, in the hands of the uninitiated, be quite catastrophic. The Primal Institute and the Primal Center, both here in Los Angeles, state that its practice is very dangerous unless the therapist has been trained at one of these institutions. Taking patients into old feelings that they are not ready for can initiate psychosis (as happened in some cases of using lysergic acid). Both the Primal Institute and the Primal Center require an extensive internship process to become a therapist. I fully concur with that.

I have not been asked nor trained to practice Primal Therapy.

Neurosis is the problem. Neurosis is the pathology (death knell) of feelings. We need to re-learn to feel, as best we can. Most of our preconceived ideas about many things need to be re-thought. Maybe it is only youth, being close enough to their childhoods and feelings, who will grasp this. Can we collectively **make a bold attempt to NOT damage our children** as much as we were, thereby reducing neurosis in the next generations?

———

I wrote this to express myself in writing, to promote the theory that I felt was the outcome of the greatest discovery of all time. Having promoted the ideas verbally over the years, I realized that most people over 25 had already become mature in their neurosis and it is hard to change their concepts, unless their old feelings are rising and their defense system is weak. I therefore dedicate this book to the children of the world and hope the youth, being closer to their feelings than most, might read it and get the "wow" factor. It was a long and arduous process over a period of more than 25 years of collecting notes and trying out my ideas and opinions (feelings) verbally in the hope that I might see a way to write and be convincing.

Primal Therapy is not advisable for everyone, unless you really feel you have no other choice. Feeling therapy should only be attempted by those who have given ***considerable*** thought to it and have read ***carefully*** what I have written. **I repeat, this is not for the casual reader.** As a species we can greatly benefit from knowing the theory and, hopefully, start a process whereby the next generation will not be as damaged as we are. Progressively, (maybe in only four or five generations) all humans could then become free from this extremely debilitating disease.

Jack's feelings in brief:

1) Neurosis is 99% of all our problems.
2) Feelings are everything; and ones true health.
3) Thinking is our first and greatest act-out.
4) Our cultures are our self-made prisons where we have incarcerated ourselves.
5) Civilization is our curse, not our redemption.
6) Learning is simple; teaching is complicated and convoluted.
7) Once the problem is truly defined, it's simple. It's the solution that is complicated.
8) Economics is the quagmire which entrapped us.
9) "Free market practices" is an oxymoron. It is anything but free.
10) Religion (believing) *is* the root of all evil.
11) To go from rules to laws, then laws to politics, then politics to money, is crazy.
12) Politicians don't have answers, only egos.
13) I feel, therefore I be (exist).
14) Childrearing is slavery: potential parents should fully understand this hardship.
15) Life's about experiencing it—billions of moments—just like now.

Glossary of Terms

Act-in: The body's attempt to do the same as the defense system and hide from pain by ultimately creating an illness to circumvent pain—a paradox.

Act-out: An action or ingestion (drugs) to defend against a rising feeling, known also as a defense.

Buddying: Two people getting together to listen to one another (one at a time) to express their feelings and thoughts on matters concerning the speaker.

Buddy: Someone who gets into buddying with you from time to time.

***Center of the Cyclone*:** A philosophical book title by John C. Lilly suggesting that thinkers both spiritual and otherwise all headed towards a central point, but that none of them seemingly got to that central point.

Dumping: In short, blaming others for ones feelings, e.g., the boss gives you a bad time and you come home and kick the dog—a dump on the dog.

Etymology: The study of the origins or derivation of words from parent languages.

Overwhelming pain: While it may seem obvious what the word overwhelming or the word pain mean, it is only when experiencing "*overwhelming pain*" we feel the gravity of it. The phrase almost defies explanation.

Primal: I use this in the context of "first" experiences (reliving) of feelings at the onset of our individual lives.

Primal Pain: Overwhelming pain laid down in our subconscious at a time of our early development from fetus to the end of childhood.

Re-living: Re-experiencing an event (usually childhood), just as it was at the time it actually occurred, as opposed to remembering that event.

Sovereign unto ourselves: Being our own personal authority to ourselves.

Subliminal: One's awareness that there is something, but not quite having full knowledge or access to it—below the threshold of consciousness.

Bibliography

The Primal Scream G. P. Putnam's Sons, 1970 by Dr. Arthur Janov

Prisoner of Pain Doubleday Press, 1980 by Dr. Arthur Janov

Primal Healing New Page Books, 2006 by Dr. Arthur Janov

A Brief History of Time Bantam Books, 1988 by Stephen W. Hawking

Cure By Crying published by the author 1995 Thomas A. Stone

Birth Without Violence Newmarket Press 1990 by Dr. Frédérick LeBoyer

Continuum Concept Perseus, 1977 by Jean Liedloff

Real Fatherhood 1st Books Library, 2002 by Bob Kamm

Center of the Cyclone New York Julian Press, 1972 by John C. Lilly

Language, Thought, and Reality, Selected Writings of Benjamin Lee Whorf M. L. T. Press, 1956 by John B. Carroll

Use of the Self E. P. Dutton 1932 Frederick Maithers Alexander